Sea Life

Barnacles

Lola Schaefer

www.raintreepublishers.co.uk
Visit our website to find out more information about **Raintree** books.

To order:
- ☎ Phone 44 (0) 1865 888112
- 📄 Send a fax to 44 (0) 1865 314091
- 💻 Visit the Raintree Bookshop at www.raintreepublishers.co.uk to browse our catalogue and order online.

First published in Great Britain by Raintree, Halley Court, Jordan Hill, Oxford OX2 8EJ, part of Harcourt Education.
Raintree is a registered trademark of Harcourt Education Ltd.

Editorial: Nick Hunter and Diyan Leake
Design: Sue Emerson (HL-US) and Joanna Sapwell (www.tipani.co.uk)
Picture Research: Amor Montes de Oca (HL-US)
Production: Lorraine Hicks

Originated by Dot Gradations
Printed and bound in China by South China Printing Company

ISBN 1 844 21010 3
07 06 05 04 03
10 9 8 7 6 5 4 3 2 1

British Library Cataloguing in Publication Data
Schaefer, Lola
Barnacles
595.3'5
A full catalogue record for this book is available from the British Library.

Acknowledgements
The publishers would like to thank the following for permission to reproduce photographs: Bruce Coleman Inc. pp. **6** (Norman Tomalin), 15R (Nicholas Devore), **23** (dock, Norman Tomalin) Color Pic, Inc. p. **4** (E. R. Degginger) Corbis p. **17** (Stuart Westmorland) Jay Ireland & Georgienne E. Bradley/Bradleyireland.com pp. **13**, **19**, **23** (feeding legs and plate), back cover (feeding legs) Jeff Rotman Photography pp. **10**, **16**, 21R Rod Barbee p. **12** Seapics.com pp. **1** (Doug Perrine), **5** (David B. Fleetham), **7** (Doug Perrine), **8** (A. Maywald), **9** (Marilyn Kazmers), **18** (Peter Parks/iq3-d), **22** (A. Maywald), **23** (invertebrate, David B. Fleetham plankton, Peter Parks/iq3-d), **24** (A. Maywald), back cover (plankton, Peter Parks/iq3-d) Visuals Unlimited p. **11** (William S. Ormerod, Jr.), 14R (David Wrobel), **20** (Triarch), 21L (John Cunningham), 14L (Peter Morris) and 15L (Corbis)

Cover photograph of barnacles, reproduced with permission of Visuals Unlimited (William S. Ormerod, Jr)

Every effort has been made to contact copyright holders of any material reproduced in this book. Any omissions will be rectified in subsequent printings if notice is given to the publishers.

 CAUTION: Remind children that it is not a good idea to handle wild animals. Children should wash their hands with soap and water after they touch any animal.

Some words are shown in bold, **like this**. You can find them in the glossary on page 23.

Contents

What are barnacles?

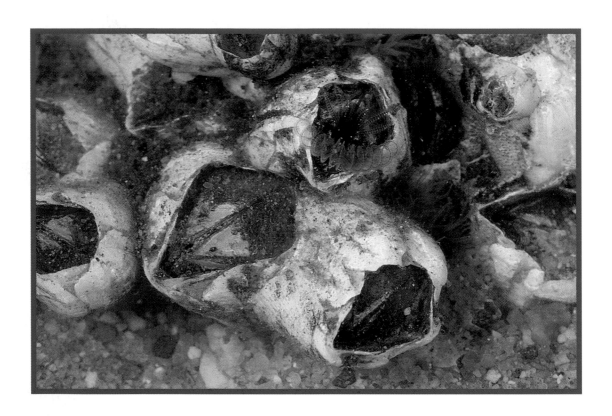

Barnacles are little animals.

They are hard on the outside.

They do not have any bones inside.

Animals that do not have backbones are called **invertebrates**.

Barnacles are invertebrates that live in the sea.

Where do barnacles live?

Barnacles may live in the water.

They may live where the sea water washes over them.

barnacles

turtle

Barnacles live on ships, **docks** and rocks.

Some barnacles live on other animals!

What do barnacles look like?

feeding legs

Barnacles look like little cones.

This barnacle's **feeding legs** are sticking out of its cone.

Barnacles can be white or red.

They can be grey or brown.

What are barnacle shells like?

People call the outsides of barnacles 'shells'.

But the outsides of barnacles are hard **plates**.

plates

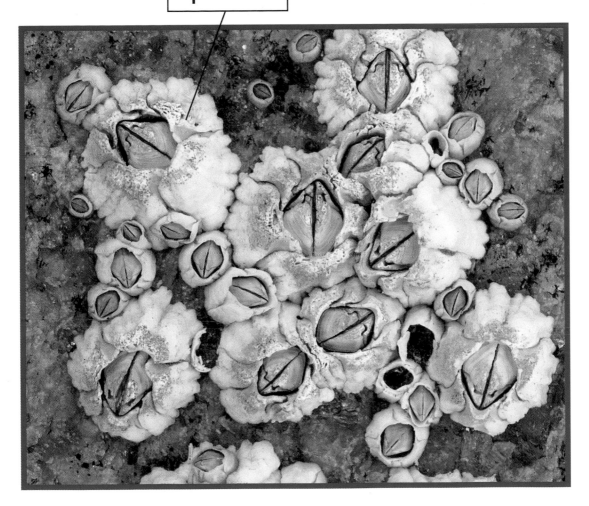

As barnacles grow, they make more plates.

The hard plates keep barnacles safe from birds and crabs.

What do barnacles feel like?

Barnacles feel hard on the outside.

Their **plates** are hard as stone.

feeding legs

Their **feeding legs** feel hairy.

How big are barnacles?

Young barnacles are as big as the head of a pin.

Some adult barnacles are as big as conkers.

How do barnacles move?

Young barnacles swim in the sea.

They stick themselves to something hard.

Then the barnacles start to grow **plates**.

When they have plates, barnacles never move.

What do barnacles eat?

Barnacles eat tiny sea plants and animals called **plankton.**

This picture makes the plankton look big.

feeding legs

The barnacle uses its **feeding legs** to catch plankton.

Then it pushes the plankton into its mouth with its legs.

Where do new barnacles come from?

Barnacles lay eggs inside their shells.

Young barnacles come out of the eggs and swim away.

Young barnacles grow and change many times.

Quiz

What are these barnacle parts?

Can you find them in the book?

Look for the answers on page 24.

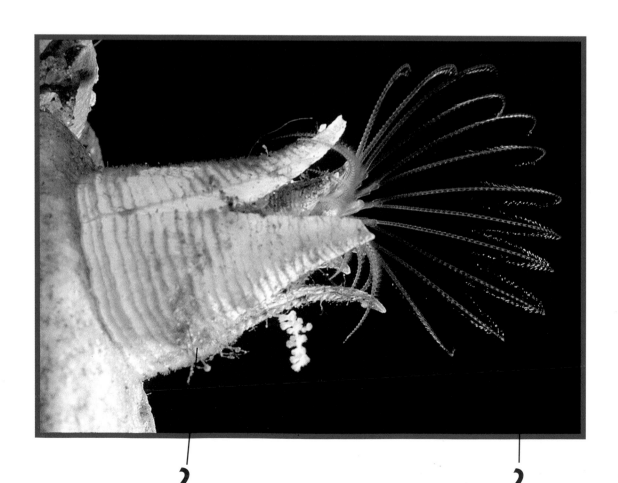

?

?

Glossary

dock
place by the sea that is built up so boats can stop there

feeding legs
a barnacle's legs, which it uses to catch food with

invertebrate
animal that has no backbone

plankton
tiny plants and animals that live in the sea

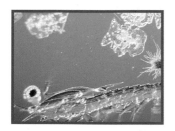

plate
the hard outside part of a barnacle

Index

animals   4, 5, 7

birds   11

backbones   5

bones   4

crabs   11

docks   7, 23

eggs   20, 23

feeding legs   8, 13, 19, 23

invertebrates   5, 23

mouths   9

plates   10, 11, 12, 17, 23

plankton   18, 19, 23

rocks   7

sea   5, 6, 16

shells   10, 20

ships   7

water   6

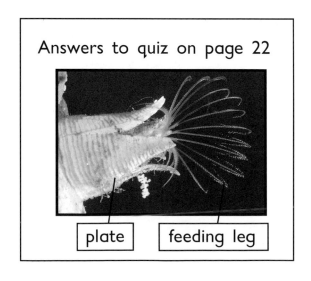

Answers to quiz on page 22

plate   feeding leg

24

Titles in the Sea Life series include:

Hardback   1 844 21010 3

Hardback   1 844 21011 1

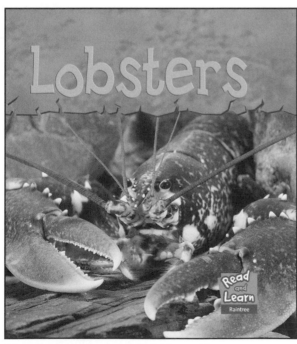

Hardback   1 844 21012 X

Hardback   1 844 21013 8

Find out about the other titles in this series on our website www.raintreepublishers.co.uk